T0012121

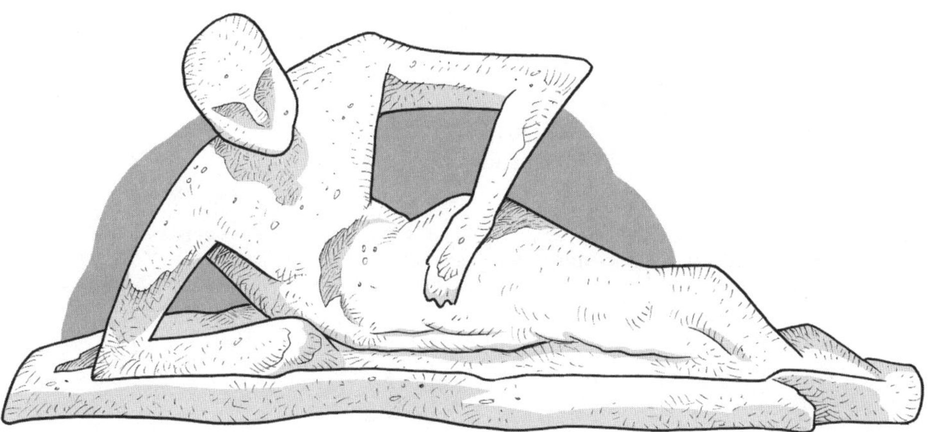

Published in Great Britain in MMXXII by
The Salariya Book Company Ltd
25 Marlborough Place, Brighton BN1 1UB
www.salariya.com

ISBN: 978-1-913971-14-4

1 3 5 7 9 8 6 4 2

A CIP catalogue record for this book is available from the British Library.
Printed and bound in Malta.

Author: Roger Canavan
Illustrator: Damian Zain
Editor: Nick Pierce

E-book version available.

ADVENTURES IN THE REAL WORLD

AD79 THE DESTRUCTION OF POMPEII

WRITTEN BY
ROGER CANAVAN

ILLUSTRATED BY
DAMIAN ZAIN

SALARIYA
Brilliant Books Make Brilliant Children

MAP OF VOLCANIC DESTRUCTION

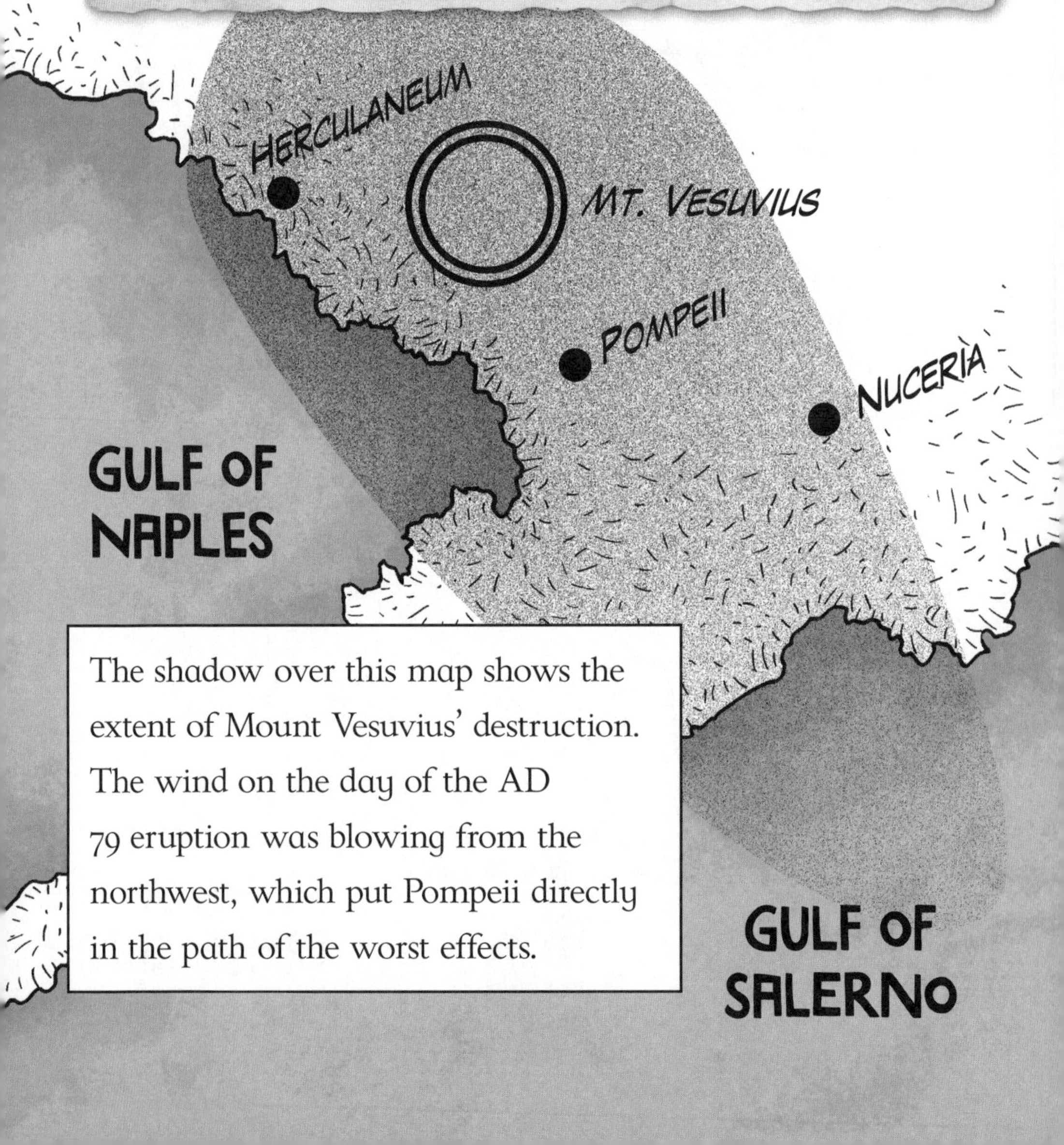

HERCULANEUM

MT. VESUVIUS

POMPEII

NUCERIA

GULF OF NAPLES

The shadow over this map shows the extent of Mount Vesuvius' destruction. The wind on the day of the AD 79 eruption was blowing from the northwest, which put Pompeii directly in the path of the worst effects.

GULF OF SALERNO

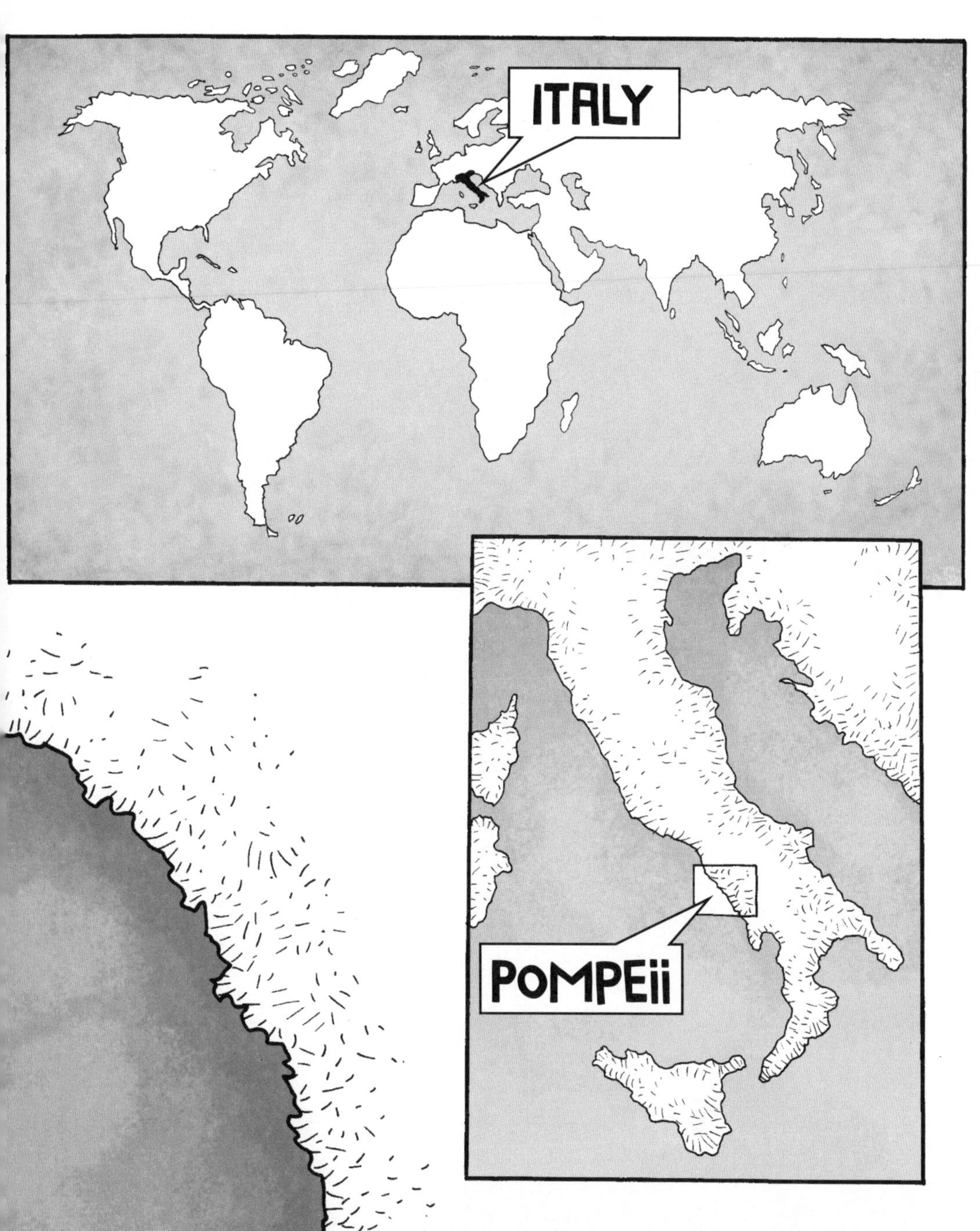

ITALY
POMPEii

INTRODUCTION

A stern-looking guard is leading a family out through a gate between two large columns. The father seems to be apologising to the guard while the mother has taken their young son aside: 'Do you know how much we paid for that phone? Last week you left it on the school bus and today we spent two hours hunting through Pompeii before we found it. And we had to ask this nice guard to stay behind after the visiting hours ended.'

Her angry voice could be heard, getting fainter and fainter, from inside the courtyard, on the other side of the gate.

A grey horse and a sleek black dog, like a slim Labrador, were chatting together in an open courtyard – part of a ruined temple. The remains of ten large columns ran along the edges of the courtyard. Each looked like the stump of a giant tree that has been cut down. The dog was resting on top of one of those columns.

'Whew! Alone at last,' said the horse, appearing from the shadows and shaking his mane back and forth. 'I thought that last family would never leave. Aren't the guards meant to usher them out?'

His dog companion replied, 'The guard was just being kind. He was helping them find the phone that the son had lost.'

'What's a phone?'

'What's a phone?! Haven't you noticed what every visitor has been carrying these past twenty years? Come on, bird brain – get with it. Things move on, you know. It's not AD 79 anymore. How many chariots do you see pulling up? Any gladiators clanking around?'

The horse neighed angrily. 'I am not a bird brain. My name is Mannulus, which means "noble fighting horse"'.

'No it doesn't. It means "pony", and you know it. I'm the one with the noble name: Lupus, as you know, means "wolf". Grrrr. Ah-oooo.'

Lupus had tried to howl like a wolf, but it sounded a bit more like a squeak. They both started laughing. But Mannulus was still feeling a bit cross about being teased over his name: 'I thought you were meant to be a guard dog. If that's how you howled when the volcano blew, then it's no wonder that people weren't warned about what was coming.'

'There you go again. And I suppose you spent the whole time going back and forth rescuing the townsfolk of Pompeii? Come to think of it, I wonder whether any of them are still around.'

The animals' mood changed again, as they became thoughtful. Mannulus spoke first: 'Those humans. Why did they ever think of building a town at the foot of a volcano?'

'Well, it's a long story.'

'I'm all ears. Well, maybe not all ears – that would make me a donkey. But I really would like to know why they took such a chance.'

POM

CHAPTER ONE

A CROSSROADS OF CULTURES

Lupus had led the pair of animal friends to the western edge of Pompeii, by the remains of the Temple of Venus. Mannulus seemed to be a little out of breath.

'I didn't know dogs could move so fast. I had to trot – or is it canter? – to keep up with you. My legs are a little sore: I haven't had this much exercise for about a thousand, no, two thousand years. I hope you've dragged me over here for a good reason.'

Lupus smiled. 'Just look.'

'All right, there's Vesuvius. Great. Is that its handsome side?'

'No, silly. You're looking the wrong way. Turn around and look west. Anything spring to mind?'

'Ahhh. Look at how the sunlight plays on the deep blue waters of the Mediterranean.'

'All right, Mister Poet. Yes, it is a beautiful view. Nowadays people call that the Bay of Naples, but you probably still know it by its Roman nickname, the Crater. Anyway, I want you to think a bit more about it. Remember how you were asking why anyone would build a town so close to an active volcano?'

Mannulus was keen to show that he knew where the conversation was leading. 'Of course. People wanted to live where they'd have a lovely ocean view.'

MY WIFE AND I ARE PLANNING ON MOVING DOWN FROM ROME AND BUILDING A COUNTRY VILLA NEAR HERE.
FINE, I'LL SHOW YOU A LOVELY SPOT.
THAT SMELL IS AWFUL!
IT'S NOT SO BAD. WE GET USED TO IT.
I SAID 'A COUNTRY VILLA', NOT A VILLA IN ANOTHER COUNTRY.
IT'S GOOD EXERCISE. YOU MIGHT EVEN FIT INTO A SLIMMER TUNIC AFTER A WHILE.

AND YOU CAN DIG YOUR LATRINE RIGHT HERE.
UGH. SO THERE'S NO PLUMBING THIS FAR OUT OF TOWN.
AND IF YOU TURN AROUND YOU'LL HAVE THE WONDERFUL VIEW OF THE BAY.
WAIT! THAT HILL UP THERE IS SMOKING.
NONSENSE. IT'S ONLY A LOW CLOUD.

'Well, that's partly true. But you're jumping ahead a little bit, to around the time of the Romans. We're trying to think of why anyone would build here in the first place. Long before the Romans showed up. Why might being close to the sea be an advantage?'

'To go swimming?'

'Do you want an explanation or not? What sort of serious activities take place by the sea?'

'Wait a minute! You're not going to trick me. We're not really by the sea – we're looking down at it. We must be 2 kilometres (1.2 miles) from the water's edge. That's a long way to go for swimming... or anything serious, as you put it.'

Lupus began to feel bad about coming across like a show-off. But he still wanted his friend to understand why Pompeii's location was so important. So instead of making Mannulus feel silly by having to answer what seemed like trick questions, he decided to explain things clearly.

'You're right. We are a good way from the sea. But the sea wasn't always so far off. In fact, at the time of the eruption it was about a quarter as far away. The extra distance was created by the huge amount of lava that has flowed down from Vesuvius. Not just from the big eruption that we knew, but from lots of others – big and small – over the years.

'So the first settlement here was much closer to the shore. And a settlement close to the sea – but not close enough to be battered by waves in a storm – could trade goods by boat with other places. In fact it could send things all across the Mediterranean.'

'And the Bay of Naples is part of the Mediterranean Sea.' Mannulus had his 'intelligent horse' expression.

'Exactly. Now the Pompeii that we remember was part of the Roman Empire and the people were Roman citizens.' Lupus had raised his paw to point out the ruins of the town and the sea. And just when he got to the word 'citizens' he lost his balance and fell into a cactus growing in a ditch. He let out a howl that probably could be heard from Vesuvius all the way out to sea.

Mannulus couldn't let that pass, so he teased his friend. 'Now that's finally a howl like a wolf. Too bad you had to get stuck with all those cactus spikes to make that noise though. Do you need some help getting out of that ditch?'

'No, thank you.' Lupus was embarrassed but relieved that his fur hid any signs of blushing. He took a deep breath and spoke again with a serious voice. 'As I was saying...'

Mannulus was still chuckling, so Lupus added in a slightly louder voice: 'As I was saying, the Pompeii that we knew was

Roman, and as in other towns and cities in the Roman Empire, the people added temples, baths and theatres to make their town like a mini-Rome.'

'And they spoke Latin, like us!' Mannulus let out a proud neigh, but it didn't sound like Latin.

'Yes, but the point I was trying to make before I was so rudely interrupted...'

'By a pesky cactus that was stinging your bottom,' Mannulus laughed.

'The point was that the Romans were only the latest group of people to settle here. In fact, the town was almost 800 years old by the time we showed up.'

'Aha. That might explain why I remember some people speaking Greek. That's not Greece on the other side of the bay, is it?'

Lupus smiled and quickly scratched a cactus sore while Mannulus gazed out to sea. 'No, that's not Greece, but people from Greece were some of the first people to build towns around the bay. In fact, they built towns all across the Mediterranean. They weren't the first people to live around this coastline, but they were the most advanced.

POMPEII'S FIRST SETTLERS

Human beings have lived in or near the Bay of Naples for many thousands of years but the first traces of civilisation in Pompeii were left by mysterious people known as the Oscans. Their settlements date from about 780 BC, but they were either absorbed or defeated by later Greek arrivals in 740 BC. Even if the Oscans left little evidence of their way of life, Roman military records suggest that their influence lasted for centuries. A major uprising against Roman rule by the Samnite people was finally crushed in 290 BC. And the language spoken by that fierce people? Oscan.

'Some of those other people were happy to trade with the Greek towns and villages springing up along the bay. Others came to view the Greeks as their enemy. Some of the earliest buildings in Pompeii were built by people known as the Etruscans. They were a bit mysterious, but we do know that they kept fighting the Greeks.

PICKING AND CHOOSING

Trade and travel within the Mediterranean region meant that Pompeii was influenced by many cultures. Like many neighbouring cities in southern Italy, it had ties with Greece. We can see the Greek influence across Pompeii, especially in the style of architecture. The theatre and many religious temples also have Greek origins. But the city remained open to other influences at the same time, and through the Roman period. Paintings, ornaments and jewellery show that Pompeiians were open to ideas and practices from Egypt and the Middle East.

'Eventually the Greeks defeated the Etruscans in this area, and Pompeii became a Greek town. Farmers soon saw that they could get rich harvests on the slopes of a certain mountain...'

Mannulus shook his mane and looked back at Vesuvius. 'And I think I know which mountain you mean!'

'That's right. They could pack their fruits and vegetables and send them the short way down the river to the port. From there they could send them to merchants across the bay – or in some cases, across the Mediterranean.'

Mannulus snorted. 'And were they the ones who started making that horrible, stinky fish sauce?'

'I think you mean garum.'

'More like garbage, if you ask me.' Mannulus wrinkled his nose as he remembered the smell of that fish sauce that became a speciality of Pompeii.

GARUM

Pompeii was inland but had links with fishing communities on the nearby coast. It became famous for producing one of the ancient world's most popular condiments: garum. This salty fish sauce had a very strong taste and smell. The odour was so strong that garum factories (where fish were cleaned and the sauce prepared) had to be on the edge of town. We would probably find it disgusting, but it found its way to homes across the Roman Empire. The precious liquid was stored in narrow-necked jars called amphorae, which were sealed with lead.

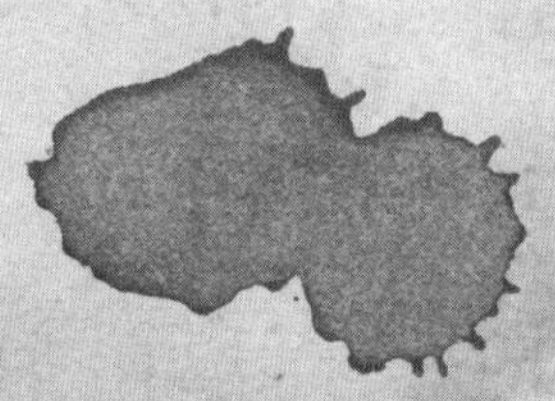

'I agree. Those humans have some funny tastes. Well, there was a busy area on the outskirts of town – not far from here – where they produced garum. Then they'd store it in those special jars called amphorae to be sent away.

'All this time Rome was becoming more powerful, all across the peninsula. For a while the Romans left Pompeii alone, and even traded with them. Pompeii became richer during this time because the merchants could send their fruit, oil and garum...' – Lupus and Mannulus said 'yuck' together at the sound of that word – 'to many other places controlled by Rome.'

'So Pompeii was a Roman town by this point?' Mannulus was still snorting a little, trying to get rid of the awful memory of garum.

'Yes and no. Let's take a walk around town, or what's left of it, to see what I mean.'

CHAPTER TWO

DAILY LIFE

The friends began a stroll through the ruins of Pompeii, which were empty again after being full of tourists all day. The early evening light cast long shadows, making Lupus and Mannulus quiet, thoughtful and at times a little sad as they remembered what life was like in the lively town. They hadn't gone more than a few paces before Mannulus stopped by the columns of a temple.

He began, 'So, let me get this right. This is the biggest place of worship in all of Pompeii.'

'That's right,' said Lupus. 'It's the Temple of Venus. You and I have waited outside it many times while our masters' families worshipped or attended festivals in honour of Venus.'

'And Venus was the goddess of Love, and Beauty, and Fertility,' continued Mannulus. Lupus was smiling patiently as he listened to his friend speak.

Mannulus looked as though he was on the verge of solving a real puzzle. 'So this temple was built to look Greek, with all those columns and statues, but it honoured a Roman goddess. That means...'

Lupus interrupted. 'What it means is that our home town, Pompeii, remained a mixture. And not just of Greek and Roman influences. Just last week I heard some visitors reading out from a guidebook. It said that the Temple of Venus was really built by the Samnites to honour their god Mephitis. And when Pompeii finally lost its independence and became another Roman colony, the locals changed the name to the Temple of Venus.'

'Why Venus? Aren't there loads of gods?' Mannulus hadn't solved the puzzle after all and still seemed confused.

'Because Venus was the favourite goddess of Sulla, the Roman general who conquered Pompeii. It would make sense to keep him happy – he might stop picking on Pompeii and find somewhere else to conquer.'

Mannulus tried to sort out the confusion, but he seemed to make things worse. 'So you and I grew up in a town that was founded by Samnites, or were they Oscans, and then Etruscans and Greeks, or was it Greeks and then Etruscans. And finally Romans. Phew!'

Lupus thought that it would be best to move on from the

Temple so that they wouldn't get tied up in knots. 'Let's stick with "finally Romans" because the daily life in Pompeii – the daily life that we can remember – was Roman, regardless of the confusing, mixed-up early history of the town. Or maybe I should say Roman with more than a splash of Greek.

'You see, the Romans admired the Greeks and they built theatres and temples and other public buildings in the Greek style. They even worshipped most of the same gods, although they gave the gods different names. That was true even in Rome itself, not just Pompeii.

'And that's pretty much how Pompeii remained right up to the time of the disastrous "big blow" from Vesuvius. In many ways it still looked like a Greek town, but its laws and government were Roman.'

Mannulus had grown quiet and was looking across at the ruins. 'It's so sad. Pompeii is silent now, but I can remember the sights and sounds of a bustling town.'

'Me too. Come on, let's take a walk through the remains to help us remember. But first, take another look out to sea and across that magnificent bay.'

VIOLENT COMBAT

As in other large communities in the Roman world, people in Pompeii had a chance to watch gladiators battle each other – sometimes to the death. Pompeii's magnificent amphitheatre was built a century before the Colosseum in Rome. Its 35 rows of seats could hold up to 20,000 spectators. Outside were booths selling refreshments and souvenirs while the outside walls had posters praising the gladiators and recording outcomes of their fights. A wall painting in one Pompeii house shows a wounded gladiator crouching and begging for mercy while his opponent holds his knife at the ready.

COME ON, WE MIGHT BE IN TIME TO SEE THE GLADIATORS!
OKAY. WHO NEEDS SCHOOL, ANYWAY?
THIS ISN'T THE AMPHITHEATRE, IT'S A TEMPLE!
QUICK, LET'S GET OUT OF HERE!
EXCUSE US, SIR. WHICH WAY TO THE GLADIATORS?
I'LL TELL YOU, BUT FIRST HELP ME UNLOAD THESE BARRELS!

THE GLADIATORS FIGHT IN THE AMPHITHEATRE, AT THE END OF THAT ROAD.

QUICK, IT'S A RACE AGAINST TIME.

WHAT A FIGHT!

THE BEST SO FAR.

TOO BAD THAT'S IT UNTIL NEXT YEAR.

OH NO, WE'VE MISSED IT!

The horse looked out, but sneaked one or two looks at Lupus to make sure that this wasn't another tease. Just to make sure, he said, 'Well, it still looks beautiful and I prefer to call it the Crater rather than the Bay of, Bay of, Bay...'

'...of Naples. That's what they call Neapolis nowadays. And they call the country Italy. You're right. It is beautiful here, and that's part of the reason that Pompeii grew. Wealthy people from Rome itself came down this way to build villas overlooking the sea, just as you said earlier. Plus, remember that Romans really respected the Greeks. Pompeii and most of the area around the Bay still felt a lot more Greek than Rome did. A rich Roman coming down here could feel almost as though he'd visited Greece. And if he had a lovely villa down here, well that would really be something to brag about back in the capital.'

By now the two friends were walking slowly again, looking around at the remains of the town that they had called home – and still did.

They had not gone far before they reached the Basilica, where business and legal matters were discussed and decided on back in Pompeii's heyday. The pair stopped and Lupus spoke.

'Many was the time that I waited outside these columns while my master conducted his business inside. Even on a quiet day it was bustling. Look at that small room on the end.'

Mannulus nodded. 'I know that room very well. It was often used as a jail. I sometimes had to take suspected criminals there in a cart. The prisoner would be guarded in that room while his case was argued inside.'

Lupus also had some memories of the Basilica. 'There's another space behind those chopped-off columns where people just hung around – lawyers with no case, teachers looking for pupils, or artists hoping that someone would hire them to paint a room.

'Some of them got bored and carved their initials on the wall or wrote some sort of message, like graffiti. My master came out once, laughing. He'd seen a message that someone had written complaining to the goddess Venus that she hadn't helped some girl fall in love with him.'

'I've heard about those bits of graffiti. There was another one that I remember. It read "I sit here alone and hungry. Pius Cossus was meant to invite me to dinner but he hasn't."'

Lupus laughed. 'I can imagine him sitting there, feeling sorry for himself. He should have given up and gone to the market in the Forum for some food. After all, it's only a few paces further. Let's go into the main Forum square.'

Mannulus looked a bit excited. 'I was never allowed in there back in the day. Everyone was afraid that I'd bump into a cart full of food or knock over a statue. Whoa! Look at the size of this square. And good old Vesuvius looking down on us from the far end.'

'I'm not so sure I'd describe Vesuvius as good. Powerful, maybe.' Lupus had joined Mannulus in the centre of the main square of Pompeii's Forum.

'That's true,' Mannulus agreed. 'Plus, back in the day you'd have a hard time even seeing Vesuvius beyond this open space. It would have been so busy with wagons and carts piled high with fruit and vegetables, plus temples with tall columns and statues standing on the empty pedestals we see now.'

'And noisy!' Lupus was also remembering the busy Forum before the dreadful eruption. 'I was always well behaved, but you'd hear dogs barking, horses snorting and neighing, and goats, sheep and chickens being brought to market. You'd also hear children laughing and screaming as they played in the crowds. It's hard to imagine now.

'And some of those smells! Do you remember where they sold the fish?'

Mannulus nodded his head up and down and tried to put a hoof to his nostrils. 'Oooh. They laid the fish out on slabs under a circular roof so the sun wouldn't beat down on it. But it still smelled so strong.'

The pair walked across the wide Forum as if they were trying to get away from the horrible fishy smell. They came to the remains of the Granary, where officials stored large amounts of grain. In times of disaster or some other crisis, the officials would open the doors to help people get food. The rich would pay a small price and the poorer people would get theirs for free.

Mannulus looked thoughtful: 'At the first signs of the eruption, when the sky darkened and ash began to fall, it would have soon been obvious that it was no ordinary crisis and that people weren't just going to stick around to queue up for food.'

Lupus was also thinking about those dark days, but his

expression quickly changed. He said 'Let's stop brooding about the eruption, at least for a while. Look – we're not far from the Stabian Baths and the Theatre. We can get to them before it becomes dark. We'll have happier memories over there.'

The pair walked slowly past a row of houses. Their walls had collapsed, leaving just the markings of where the rooms were. Wealthier merchants would have lived in some of the larger houses but there were smaller dwellings alongside them. Soon they reached the well-preserved Stabian Baths, the largest baths in Pompeii.

'Quick,' Lupus suggested, 'let's go inside before the light fades, now that the human visitors have gone. This is one place where dogs and horses weren't allowed and I've always been curious to see inside.

'I knew that everyone in Pompeii went to one of the baths regularly, partly to get clean but also to meet friends, plan dinners or just gossip. I knew the routine. First the bathers would get rubbed down with oil and then they might go outside to get some exercise. Then back into the building to go through the different rooms.'

BATHS

With nothing like modern bathrooms in most Pompeiian houses, the public baths were necessary for hygiene. Many people, of course, used them as meeting places and an excuse to chat with their friends. Pompeii had three large public baths. Originally all three baths were fed with water from the river Sarno and local wells. As they became more popular, calling for more water, they were served by the aqueduct that brought water down from nearby hills. Each bath had three sections: a caldarium (hot bath), tepidarium (luke-warm bath, where most people washed) and the frigidarium (cold bath).

Mannulus was listening, but also admiring some of the preserved paintings on the walls and the comfortable benches along each wall. It might have been comfortable for humans, but it was no place for a horse to sit, as Mannulus found out: 'I can picture my master sitting here, getting one of his servants to scrape the oil off him with that metal scraper...'

'...called a strigil,' Lupus added. 'My master never let anyone else clean him, so he used the strigil himself. Think of how many business deals, dinner parties and political plans were plotted in these rooms.'

'That's for sure. Look, I'm beginning to bump into things because it's so dark. Let's visit one more thing, the Theatre, before nightfall.' Mannulus admired the Baths but he wanted some fresh air.

They left the Baths and continued to the southern edge of town, where the curving rows of seats of the Theatre followed the slope down to the stage.

Lupus observed, 'I can see that they saved money and time making the Theatre by building it on this hillside.'

THEATRE

Pompeii's main theatre, with rows of sloping seats, was built into the natural slope of a hill in the second century BC. Audiences of up to 5,000 came to dramatic performances. The seats nearest the stage, known as the ima, were reserved for local officials and the wealthy, and had the most leg room. A wall divided this section from the media (where the less important sat) and the summa, where the poorest spectators sat furthest from the stage. The theatre is still used for concerts, opera and plays.

'The humans might have saved some time and effort, but horses were needed to pull wagons piled high with the stones,' said Mannulus. The Theatre had been built more than a hundred years before Mannulus had been born, but he felt he should defend the horses who helped build it.

'Well, it was a real success,' Lupus noted. 'Nearly half of Pompeii's population could sit here for some of the most popular plays. And the people in the top rows could still hear everything that the actors said.'

CHAPTER THREE

THE SHADOW OF VESUVIUS

It was the next morning, several hours after sunrise. Mannulus and Lupus had just woken up, and it seems as though they had fallen asleep before they'd even left the Theatre. But before they could hide themselves again – they were worried about being taken away to some museum – they heard human voices below them.

The voices came from down on the stage. It seemed to be a group of visitors on a guided tour of Pompeii. Lupus and Mannulus had nowhere to hide, so they just stood still where they were, not making any noise and hoping that the humans wouldn't notice them and just move on.

The guide's voice became clearer: 'And Vesuvius isn't the only hillside in the area. The Pompeians, like the Romans and the Greeks before them, used the natural slope of hillsides like this one to help build their theatres. Apart from being cheaper, the slope helped the sound of the voices carry to the very last row. Look, if those statues of the horse and dog up there were alive, they'd hear me speaking. Hello Mr Horse and Mr Dog! Are you enjoying the tour so far?' The group of visitors laughed at the very idea of talking statues.

Lupus and Mannulus tried to keep still and not shake with laughter. Mannulus whispered, 'So they think we're statues that were part of the Theatre.'

'Well, we're safe for now. Let's not give the game away,' Lupus added under his breath. 'But wouldn't it be fun to secretly tag along behind that group to hear what they know about the old days?'

'Hmm. A bit risky, but I agree that it would be fun to hear what today's "experts" think. Shhh. I think he's started again.'

The guide's voice drifted upwards once more. 'It's one thing to take advantage of the slopes to build a theatre. Anyone could see why that's a good idea. But there's a big, big mystery about Pompeii: why would people choose to build and live in a town so close to an active volcano in the first place?'

Mannulus and Lupus looked hard at each other. Their expressions seemed to say 'That's what I'd like to know.' Below them the tour leader was guiding the group from the theatre up one of the streets lined with excavated houses. Mannulus and Lupus waited for them to get far enough ahead so that they could follow the group without being noticed.

The group had stopped, so the two friends hid by the base of a grand statue. The tour leader's voice carried down to them.

'We'll be talking a lot about that mountain behind me, the active volcano called Vesuvius. It's part of an area of regular volcanic activity in the southern Italian region known as Campania. The Bay of Naples, which Vesuvius overlooks, is at the heart of this "Campanian Volcanic Arc". Some of the volcanoes in this area are dormant, meaning that they have not erupted for many years.

'Others, like Vesuvius, regularly send out plumes of gases and ash, and could erupt violently with very little notice. Scientists have also identified several undersea volcanoes, south of Naples. At first they believed all of them to be extinct (no longer active), but at least one of them does seem to be growing bigger.'

Mannulus was fascinated by this overheard lecture, but he had become annoyed by a wasp flying around his head. The guide was saying something about volcanic eruptions and earthquakes. He was explaining how the area constantly seems active with either puffs of smoke from volcanoes or little earthquakes, called tremors: 'Sometimes cups and plates shake for a moment or two, and that's that.'

STILL ACTIVE

Much of Italy lies at the junction of plates – large sections of the Earth's surface that slide around slowly. Sometimes they collide to trigger earthquakes or volcanic eruptions. Vesuvius rises above one of those junctions. Scientists have found evidence of eight major eruptions of Vesuvius in the last 17,000 years. Since 1631 Vesuvius has been in a period of steady activity, with lava flows and eruptions of ash and mud. A 1944 eruption, during the Second World War, destroyed aircraft and a nearby air base. It is impossible to predict when the next major eruption will occur.

The wasp was really bothering Mannulus, and Lupus was worried that his friend would neigh angrily, giving the game away. He put his paw to his mouth to signal 'be quiet'. Mannulus nodded, but just then the wasp stung him in the neck. Mannulus didn't bellow but he jerked his head back in pain, knocking the statue so that it began to rock.

The rocking statue caught the guide's attention, and he pointed it out to the group: 'Look! We seem to be having a tremor right now – it's making that statue shake back and forth. That's odd, because nothing seems to be shaking over by us. It must be a very localised tremor.'

Silence fell over the ruins of Pompeii. The guide and tourists stared hard at the statue as it slowly stopped swaying. At the same time, Mannulus and Lupus stood perfectly still behind the base of the statue, not daring to move or make even the slightest sound.

GRAPES GROW ON THESE VINES AS IF BY MAGIC.
HMMM. THOSE GRAPES SEEM TO BE SWINGING BACK AND FORTH.

AND EMPERORS IN ROME PRAISE THE WINE FROM POMPEII.
HOLD IT STEADY. IT'S SHAKING.

I THINK I'LL TAKE THIS HOME TO SQUEEZE ON MY DINNER INSTEAD OF THAT AWFUL GARUM.

ALWAYS TALKING ABOUT FOOD. WAS THAT YOUR TUMMY RUMBLING??

TH-TH-THAT WASN'T MY TUMMY. IT WAS THE MOUNTAIN!

Finally the statue stood motionless once more. The two friends were still holding their breath as they heard the familiar voice of the guide: 'Well, my friends. That was just a little hint of what the unstable ground beneath us can produce. We've just experienced a tremor, a pretty frequent event near any active volcano.' At that point he stepped back so that the visitors could have a better view of Vesuvius. A thin wisp of smoke was rising from its peak and some of the visitors shuddered and looked worriedly at each other.

The tour group began chatting again and walking on ahead. They were heading north through the town, with Vesuvius visible ahead of them the whole time. Mannulus and Lupus waited until it was safe and then followed them, zig-zagging through Pompeii's back streets.

'They're heading for the volcano. Do you suppose the guide knows what he's doing?' Mannulus asked. 'Ever since that eruption Vesuvius gives me the creeps.'

'Stay calm. I don't think they have time to go right up to the volcano,' Lupus answered. 'Look, he's stopping now by Vesuvius Gate, on the edge of town.'

The tour guide had led the visitors to the top of a tall wall at the edge of Pompeii. He pointed to the west, out to the Bay of Naples: 'Earlier I asked you to consider why anyone would build a settlement at the foot of a volcano like the one looking down at you. You'll get part of the answer if you look out to sea. Thousands of tourists come each year to appreciate that grand view.

'With the bay and the mountains and the warm, sunny climate it's easy to see why this area is so popular with holidaymakers today. Well, the Romans weren't that different. Some of them came down this way because it had a strong Greek tradition – and the Romans really admired the Greeks. And many of them fell in love with the whole area and decided to build villas here and in Herculaneum, closer to the coast.

'That helps explain why the Romans were so happy to settle here, but don't forget that Pompeii had been around for centuries beforehand.'

Lupus and Mannulus had stopped in the shade of a tree across the cobbled street from the tour group standing on the tower. Lupus was becoming impatient listening to the tour guide: 'That man loves the sound of his own voice. I would be much better as a tour guide. Just sit on your haunches, Mannulus, and I'll continue where he left off. Be honest: tell me who's the better tour guide.'

'What if I think that human is better? After all, the group seems to be hanging on his every word.'

'Nonsense. You and I are locals. I'm a natural leader. Remember how I led a pack of wild dogs away from the Forum and down to Herculaneum?'

'That was nearly two thousand years ago. Plus, you weren't

really explaining anything to those dogs, just chasing them away from the market.'

Lupus put on an important expression and began: 'Ladies and gentlemen...'

Mannulus started laughing and rolled over on to his side. 'Just get on with it. This isn't a speech!'

Lupus began again, this time more naturally: 'The lovely view of the Bay wasn't the main reason that the first people built a town here. Instead, it was that mountain that attracted them.' Lupus was pointing at Vesuvius. 'They knew that it was different from most hills and mountains, because of the smoke that rose from it constantly, but they also found something very special about the land around it.

'That soil on the hillside is very, very rich. The first farmers around here found that crops thrived in it. They harvested grains like barley and wheat, olives and many types of fruit.

Many of the hillsides were planted with vines, and the grapes from Pompeii produced wine that became famous across the Mediterranean.

'And all of those crops, plus the garum that people produced in Pompeii, could be sent down to the sea by boats travelling on the River Sarno.'

Lupus had an audience of one, but Mannulus was a good listener, plus he knew about this subject. He had to interrupt: 'Yes, the crops grew as if by magic, except I've heard that the real reason was that the lava from all those eruptions created a very rich soil.'

'I was going to say that,' said Lupus. He was a little annoyed by the interruption. 'While we're on the subject of Vesuvius, I should point out that volcanic eruptions and earthquakes are related. If you have one, you sometimes have the other.'

'And that's exactly what happened seventeen years before the main eruption of Vesuvius!' exclaimed Mannulus. 'I get it. That earlier earthquake, which really damaged Pompeii and Herculaneum, could almost have been a warning that a big eruption was due.'

RICH SOIL

It might seem strange to plant crops on the slope of a smoking volcano, but farmers have done that next to Vesuvius for thousands of years. The reason is simple – volcanic soil is rich in nutrients such as nitrogen and phosphorus, which help plants to grow well. Each eruption, large or small, enriches the soil even more. The soil near Vesuvius supported – and continues to support – the healthy harvest of grapes, olives and many other fruits and vegetables.

Lupus wasn't happy to have this latest interruption. 'If you're so good, why don't you be the guide?' And he sat down, sulking. As he did, he knocked a rock, which tumbled and crashed down on to the cobbled road between the animal friends and the tour group.

EARLY WARNING

Both Pompeii and neighbouring Herculaneum – towns that would be destroyed in the AD 79 eruption – were badly damaged in an earthquake in February of AD 62. Scientists now know of the close link between earthquakes and volcanic activity. That means that the earlier quake was a signal that Vesuvius would soon erupt, but local people either ignored the warning, failed to connect earthquakes with eruptions, or felt that they were powerless to protect themselves against the anger of their gods.

'What was that?' someone shouted. 'It came from up by that tree. Wait! Look! It's those two statues that we saw back at the Theatre. What are they doing here?'

Lupus and Mannulus were frozen in position, not daring to move, or even breathe.

ESCAPE ROUTES?

Pompeii had trade and transport links with nearby Herculaneum and other settlements along the great bay. As in other communities in the Roman world, the streets and roads in Pompeii and leading to neighbouring towns were paved. Road-makers used blocks of lava as paving stones. Traders could send their horse-drawn carts and wagons along these routes to and from Pompeii. And they could well have been lifesavers for those Pompeiians able to make their escape at the first signs of an eruption.

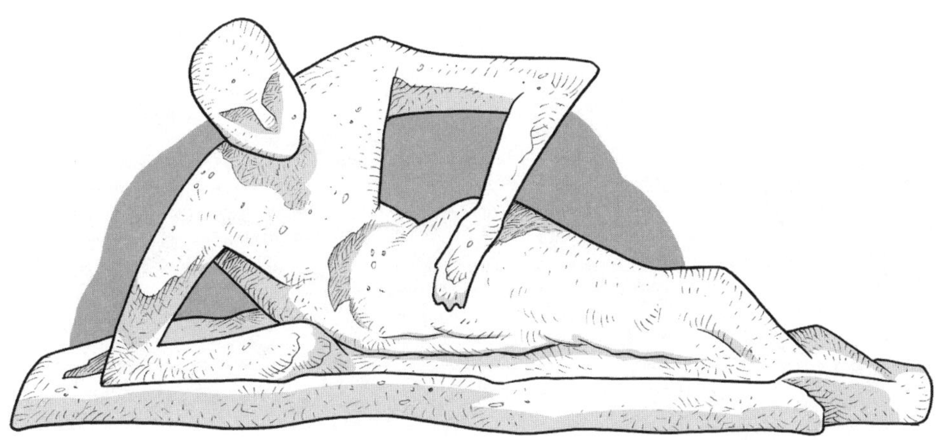

CHAPTER FOUR

FIRE FROM THE SKY

Lupus and Mannulus thought it best to remain exactly where they were until the group of tourists and their leader moved away. Vesuvius seemed that bit closer after all the talk of earthquakes and tremors and eruptions.

Mannulus broke the silence. 'You know, it doesn't feel as though all that happened two thousand years ago.'

'No. I can remember it clearly. That talk about earthquakes being a warning really got me. I wonder whether we could have done something – anything – to warn the people about the terrible eruption. Do you remember how we felt a series of small earthquakes – the type that the man called tremors – in the days leading up to the eruption?'

'Hmm. You're right. I remember those. And the gaps between them got shorter and shorter. Don't you think the humans noticed those as well? Or is it true that we animals can pick up those signals when they can't?'

Lupus tried to make them both feel a little better. 'Don't feel so bad. We sense those tremors all the time and it's not as if each one leads to a volcanic eruption. Back in AD 79 the people probably thought that the biggest risk came from another earthquake. After all, Vesuvius hadn't erupted during anyone's lifetime. And there had been the big earthquake 17 years earlier.'

'So I suppose that's why the eruption took the people in Pompeii by surprise.'

Mannulus had a dreamy expression, and it was as if he'd been sent back in time to that dreadful day: 'Yes, that day started out so peacefully, like so many others. My family's villa was just outside the city walls and the sun was streaming into the stable as I woke up. I thought it would be just the day for a ride down to the sea. Even pulling a cart to market would be enjoyable under that blue sky.'

Lupus had drifted into the same dreamy mood: 'Our house was right in the heart of Pompeii, not far from the Forum. The children were the first to wake up and they were tossing a ball back and forth in the morning sunshine. They wanted to enjoy themselves before picking up their slates and heading off to their lessons.'

Mannulus recalled, 'I had been harnessed to the wagon and we had gone up the slope to the vineyard. Several young farm workers were loading baskets of grapes on to the wagon while I grazed by some trees nearby.

'What we didn't know – who could know? – was that a massive amount of molten rock had been stirred up beneath the Earth's surface. Those earlier tremors were caused by the pressure of that liquid rock trying to find a way out. The biggest passage upwards was through Vesuvius. But a thick plug of rock in the heart of the volcano blocked the way out. And the pressure just kept on building. None of us knew it, but that plug was going to be blown sky high by the pressure.'

Lupus was nodding. 'And that plug being blown off meant the start of the eruption. If you were near Vesuvius, then you must have seen that moment. It must have been scary.'

Mannulus nodded. 'You're right. In the early afternoon the workers stopped suddenly and pointed up at Vesuvius. An enormous black cloud darkened the blue sky above it. And the cloud was moving towards Pompeii.'

Lupus got excited. 'Yes, yes. Remember Pliny the Younger's eyewitness account of the eruption? He was safe on the other side of the great bay, but he could see the events unfold. He saw that great cloud develop after the eruption began. I've heard scientists say that it rose 15 km (9.3 miles) into the atmosphere. It was a mixture of gases, ash and pumice, which is a mixture of lava and water.'

PLINY THE ELDER – AND YOUNGER

Pliny the Elder was one of the most famous people in the Roman Empire. He was a politician, military commander, author and scientist. At the time of the eruption he was based in the naval port of Misenum, on the northern shore of the Bay of Naples. The younger Pliny, his nephew, was aged seventeen or eighteen at the time and greatly admired his uncle. He was living in his uncle's house at Misenum at the time of the eruption, which adds accuracy and sadness to his account. His account of the eruption records his own observations as well as reports of his uncle's heroic efforts to save people caught up in the disaster.

'Pliny had a great eye for detail,' Mannulus agreed. 'He said that the cloud resembled "an umbrella pine tree, for it rose to a great height on a sort of trunk and then split off into branches".'

Lupus was nodding again, and he interrupted Mannulus: 'I heard that guide tell the visitors that Vesuvius was pumping one and a half million tons of volcanic matter into the sky every second!!'

Mannulus let that fact sink in, then he continued, 'The wind blew that deadly cloud towards Pompeii. It didn't take long to travel those 8 km (5 miles). We still don't know how many of the 15,000 people managed to escape before the cloud arrived. They would have had to speed about 15 km (9.3 miles) east. I saw many do that, racing away on horseback or with wagons. Others travelled down to the coast and tried to sail away from the disaster.'

IS IT JUST ME
OR IS IT GETTING
DARK OUTSIDE?

MY EYES ARE
BEGINNING TO STING.
I WONDER WHY?

MINE TOO.
I FEEL WARM.

I'VE NEVER SEEN VESUVIUS LOOK LIKE THAT. I DON'T LIKE IT. LET'S HEAD FOR THE SEA, FAST!

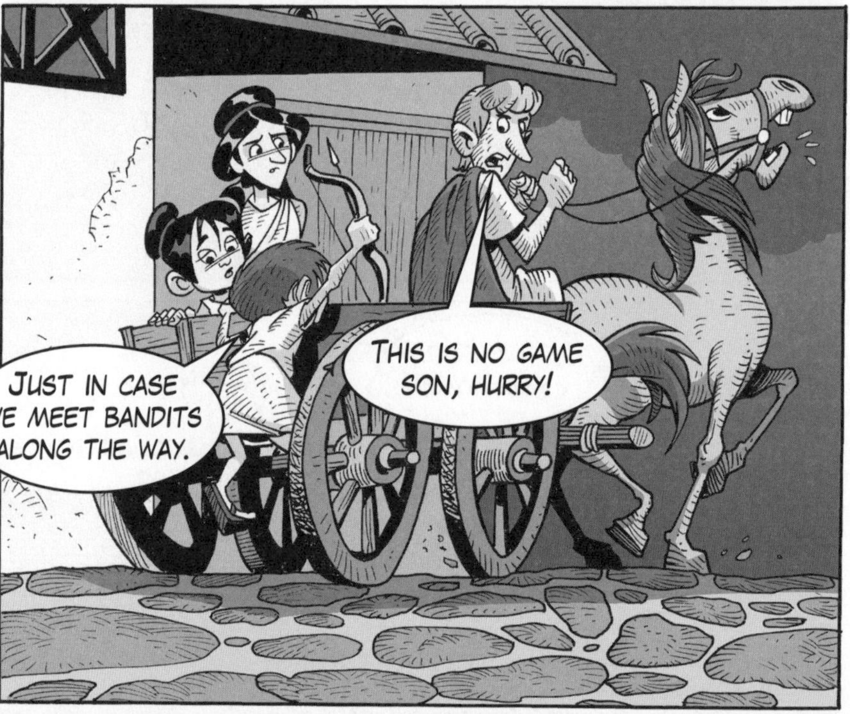

JUST IN CASE WE MEET BANDITS ALONG THE WAY.

THIS IS NO GAME SON, HURRY!

UNFINISHED BUSINESS

Peeling off the layers of ash and lava has shown just how suddenly the worst of the catastrophe struck Pompeii. Although residents had a bit of warning – in the form of dark clouds and some ash falling to the ground – the real destruction seems to have taken many people by surprise. Guard dogs have been found still chained to house entrances. Their fleeing owners would have forgotten their pets in the rush. Paint pots and brushes have been found in one house; the decorators had dropped their tools and fled.

Lupus noted, 'Some think that only about 2,000 people remained when the cloud reached Pompeii. It seems strange that many in the city had made their escape when they saw warning signs, while others seem to have carried on as if it had been just another day, but with a dark storm cloud threatening them all. People were putting up election posters, preparing to redecorate their houses and generally behaving as they normally would.

'For those poor people, dogs and horses who stayed behind, there was no escape. It must have seemed like the end of the world. Most people tried to shelter inside their houses, as if they were keeping dry in a severe thunderstorm. In fact, it must have seemed like a dreadful storm because the collision of ash and magma (hot melted rock) created lightning.

'Even the strong houses of Pompeii offered no real protection against the tons of ash and lava that poured down on the town. Gases, water, lava and ash mixed high up in the air and hardened into stone as they cooled, then fell. The poor people huddled inside were crushed when roofs collapsed on them. And those who weren't crushed, suffocated instead – unable to breathe air through the burning clouds of ash that swirled around and settled.'

Mannulus and Lupus were both now looking back at the remains of Pompeii. Their voices were a mixture of sadness and fear.

Lupus spoke first. 'And that wasn't the last of it. Eventually the column of magma inside the volcano collapsed. That triggered a series of lava avalanches that raced down the slopes at speeds of up to 100 kph (62 mph). No one, not even the fastest horse, could have outrun this deadly flow. The first of these flows stopped just before the city walls but anyone near it would have choked because of the deadly gases coming from it. Other flows would sweep down through Pompeii, crushing anything in their way.

'By the time that cloud passed, it had buried Pompeii under more than 10 metres (33 feet) of debris. It was as if a thick blanket had covered the city completely.'

Once more the pair of friends became silent. Mannulus turned his gaze from the remains of Pompeii near them and towards the sea. 'The town of Herculaneum lies down there by the sea. You can see how the excavations are revealing it once more. Like Pompeii it was buried during that eruption, but there were some big differences between them.'

'For one thing,' Lupus added, 'far more people in Herculaneum survived the disaster.'

'And horses. And dogs.' Mannulus wanted his friend to know that he also remembered the story of how the eruption affected the prosperous seaside neighbour of Pompeii. 'The main reason why so many people survived was because of the wind. On the day of the eruption, the wind was blowing in a south-easterly direction. That meant that Pompeii, which is south-east of Vesuvius, was in the firing line.'

'How do you know all this?' Lupus asked. He liked to think of himself as the clever one.

HERCULANEUM

Pompeii's neighbour Herculaneum also lay buried and largely forgotten for hundreds of years. The name Herculaneum is evidence of its earlier Greek history: it was named after the mythical Greek hero Heracles (known to us as Hercules). Herculaneum was smaller than Pompeii, but its inhabitants were richer. The coastal setting of the town made it popular with wealthy Romans who built many lavish villas overlooking the bay. Herculaneum escaped the first wave of damage in the eruption because it was further west than Pompeii. The real damage came the next day when the town (by now largely deserted) was covered with lava.

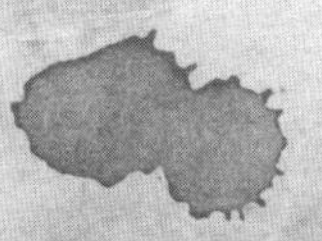

'I also listen when scientists and historians pass through here. After all, we've had about 150 years' worth of those talks to absorb.' Mannulus felt that he had made his point, and he continued calmly, 'Herculaneum lay to the west of the cloud of ash and lava that drifted down to Pompeii.'

'I get it,' Lupus quickly added, to show that he had also understood all that scientific and historical stuff. 'Unlike Pompeii, which was covered with debris from the huge cloud, Herculaneum suffered very little fall of volcanic debris from above. Only a few centimetres.'

Mannulus then pointed out something just as important: 'All of that dark-cloud bombardment lasted about 12 hours. Most of the people in Herculaneum must have decided that another cloud might head their way, so they made their escape, mainly by sea.

'But it's that second stage – the fast-flowing lava – that was the other big difference with Pompeii. And in a way that tells us more about why Herculaneum is better preserved than its more famous neighbour.'

THE WRONG DATE?

A phrase in Pliny the Younger's account suggested that the eruption took place on 'nonum kal. Septembres', which would be 24 August. But other evidence now suggests that Vesuvius erupted in the autumn. Pomegranates and walnuts (which ripen in the autumn) have been found in the ruins. Also, archaeologists have found a charcoal inscription describing events in October of the same year. Was Pliny wrong? Probably not. His original letter has long been lost and what we have now is a copy of a copy of a version that might not have translated his words accurately.

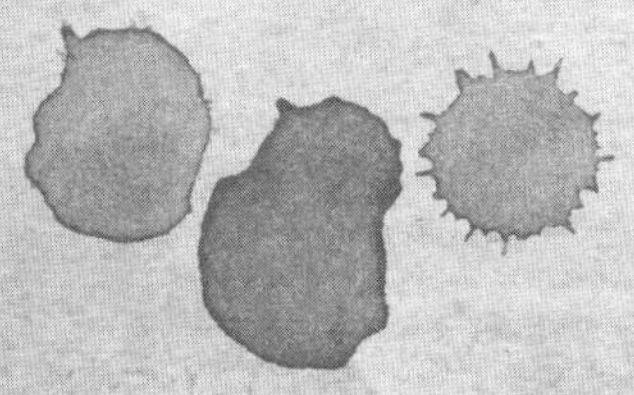

Lupus was thinking hard, eager to keep up. 'Yes, it was the second stage, with wave after wave of lava flowing down, that affected Herculaneum. The force of that flow did crush or knock over some buildings and statues, but in most of the town the flow just rose and rose, inside buildings and out.'

'A bit like a bath filling with water,' Mannulus observed.

'Yes. Many buildings remained preserved beneath the ash and lava, which in some cases created a blanket more than 20 metres (66 feet) deep.'

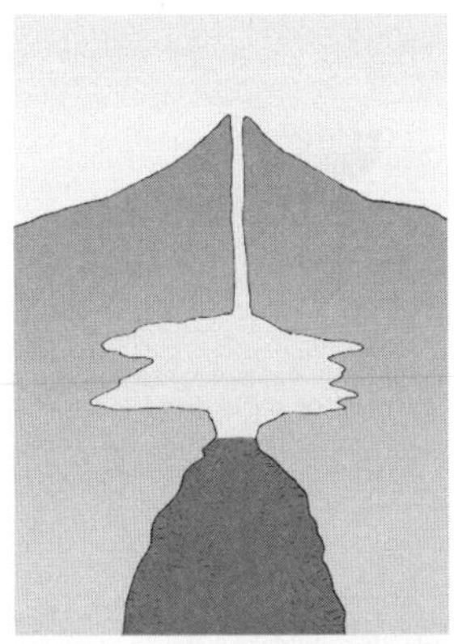

1. MAGMA CHAMBER. A SPACE UNDERNEATH MOUNT VESUVIUS HAS FILLED UP WITH MOLTEN ROCK OR MAGMA. IT'S UNDER GREAT PRESSURE.

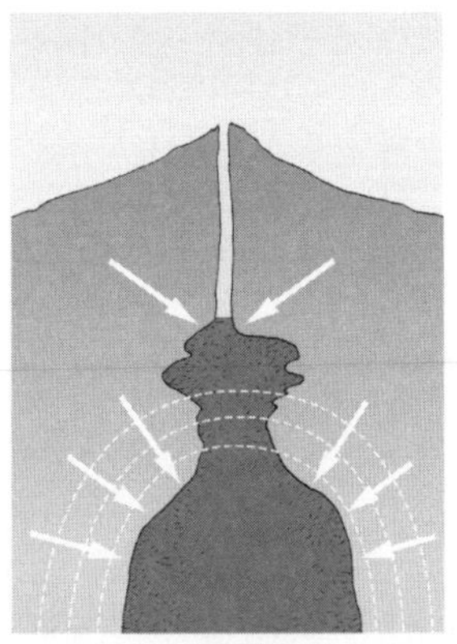

2. MAGMA RISES. AS THE PRESSURE INCREASES, THE MAGMA IS FORCED OUT OF THE CHAMBER AND UP TOWARDS THE SURFACE ALONG A CONDUIT OR PIPE.

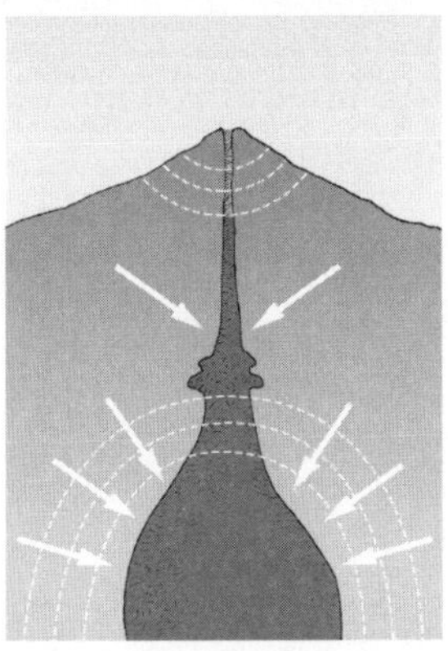

3. PUMICE. NEAR THE TOP OF THE CONDUIT, THE RED-HOT MAGMA COOLS AND MIXES WITH GASES TO MAKE PUMICE, A LIGHTWEIGHT ROCK FILLED WITH AIR BUBBLES.

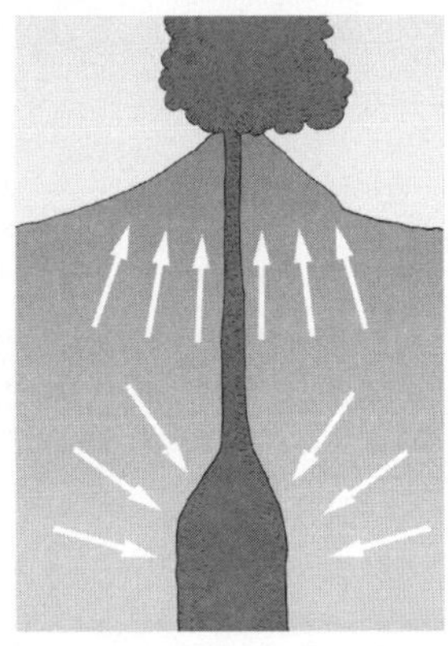

4. EXPLOSION. A HIGH-SPEED JET OF GAS RUSHES ALONG THE CONDUIT AND FORCES THE PUMICE AND TONNES OF GREY ASH INTO THE SKY.

POM

CHAPTER FIVE

LOST TO HISTORY?

‘Things got very quiet around here in the days and years that followed the eruption, didn’t they?’ Mannulus asked Lupus as the two of them returned to Vesuvius Gate, with its view over the remains of Pompeii.

‘Well, you can hardly blame people for avoiding the whole area. After all, the eruption had dumped lava and ash not just on Pompeii and Herculaneum, but on the entire Sarno Valley leading to the sea. Without a busy port and with towns and farmland buried under lava, there wasn't much to attract people.' Lupus could remember that quiet period in Pompeii's history very clearly.

Mannulus was still keen to show off his wider knowledge of the eruption and its aftermath, gained from listening to years and years of lectures and tours through the remains. He even knew that scientists and historians didn't always agree on everything about the subject. 'You know, Lupus, until recently people thought that the world forgot about Pompeii and Herculaneum completely, until they were re-discovered several hundred years ago.'

'Well, you and I know that's not quite true, don't we?' Lupus, like Mannulus, had watched over the scene since the eruption. They were pleased to see it full of life again, with its many thousands of visitors, but they also knew that the site had never been completely empty for very long.

Lupus had also been listening to the experts. Like Mannulus, he combined his own memories with other people's accounts and the latest thinking. 'We all know about Pliny the Younger's first-hand description of the eruption. Well, the famous Roman historian Suetonius gave a good account of what happened soon after the disaster.

A PRESERVING BLANKET?

Some of the ash that fell on buildings and people in Pompeii was light enough to cover them without crushing them. It settled in much the same way that snow covers a lawn or a house, growing deeper and deeper. Over many years, rainwater seeped into this layer, causing it to harden around the buried buildings and victims. The water also reacted with chemicals in the ash and lava to create a mixture that ate away at once-living substances like the victims' bodies. That left cavities (gaps) within the outer layer – hollow spaces in the shape of those bodies. Non-living material like the stone used for buildings remained unaffected by that water mixture.

'Suetonius was only ten years old when Vesuvius erupted but he collected records and interviewed people to get a full picture. Some of his accounts are very interesting. It turns out that the emperor at the time of the eruption – '

'Emperor Titus,' piped up Mannulus.

DID ANYONE SURVIVE?

Pliny the Younger's account of the eruption is an excellent description of the event itself. Modern scientists find that his details match the records of recent eruptions. But it's hard to find first-hand accounts of those who might have escaped the disaster. However, people are now finding evidence that some Pompeiians did escape before the first deadly wave. Items such as shrines and statues found locally have links with Pompeii, and they date from after the eruption. Gravestones and other inscriptions found elsewhere show names that were common in Pompeii but less so outside its walls.

'Yes, Titus. Um, the Emperor thought that the cities might be rebuilt. He found out the names of victims who had died without heirs. He then wanted their unclaimed money to be used for rebuilding.'

Mannulus observed, 'Well, as you can see there wasn't much rebuilding. Maybe because they'd also have had to rebuild all the roads, dig new fields for crops and build new harbours. It was probably too much. Plus, who wants to move into a town that was flattened by an earthquake and then buried by a volcano in the space of twenty years? But people did return, mainly survivors who hoped to find some of their previous goods beneath the ash.'

'And not just returning Pompeians,' said Lupus. 'Other people, including dishonest thieves, came to find what they considered to be buried treasure. They dug tunnels running this way and that, hoping to come across jewels and gold buried there.'

'Yes, looters. I've heard people saying that the tombs and

temples of ancient Egypt were looted in the same way. People sneak in without thinking of what they're damaging along the way and then make off with whatever they think is valuable.' Mannulus felt protective about his master's family and the others who lived in Pompeii at the time of the eruption.

'Still, the memory of these places did fade after a few hundred years. And that's partly because people stopped speaking Latin. Those records of Pliny the Younger and Suetonius gathered dust or were lost. Some people might have heard about Pompeii but thought it was just a legend, like Atlantis. But most of the barbarians who came later probably just forgot about it.' Lupus felt strongly that the world took a giant step backwards after the Roman period. For him, the Middle Ages – the years from about AD 450 to 1500 – were primitive.

It was only in the Renaissance, the period up to about 1600, that Europe became civilised again, according to this view. Why? Because people began taking an interest in ancient Greece and Rome.

'All right, Mannulus.' Lupus wanted to show that he had the best information about Pompeii. 'How did pasta help Pompeii get rediscovered?'

'Is this a riddle? I don't know, how did pasta help Pompeii to get rediscovered?'

'In 1592, Count Muzio Tuttavilla decided that his pasta factories in Torre Annunziata (by the bay) needed more water. He hired the famous architect Domenico Fontana to build an underground canal that would take water from the River Sarno. The canal passed beneath Pompeii, but the workmen only found out when they started to uncover parts of buildings and statues.

'Fontana probably knew what they had stumbled upon, but he ordered his men to cover those finds again.'

'Why?' asked Mannulus.

'We can't be sure. Some people say that he saw paintings of naked people. Others are convinced that he was trying to keep the find secret so that looters wouldn't ruin it. At any rate, the public didn't know that there had been this big discovery, even though workmen did see inscriptions with part of the word "Pompeii" written on them.

CHANGING ATTITUDES

The first excavation of Pompeii in 1592 was accidental. Domenico Fontana didn't want his men wasting their time on it, so he had them bury the evidence. The organised excavations that began in the mid-1700s uncovered thousands of objects and parts of many houses and public buildings. Diggers destroyed wall paintings and other traces of Pompeii as they rushed to find vases, urns and other objects that could be taken away and sold. In addition to pickaxes and spades, workmen even used gunpowder to blast away the layers of lava. The appointment of Giuseppe Fiorelli as director of excavations in the 1860s put an end to those destructive methods of excavating.

'It took another 150 years or so for the real re-discovery to take place. A team working for King Charles III of Naples, ruler of the area, had uncovered the remains of Herculaneum. Some of its buildings were well preserved. This work on Herculaneum had continued for ten years before Charles sent a team in 1748 to excavate a site higher up and further from the sea.'

'We know that site was Pompeii but the workmen weren't sure.' Mannulus had listened as patiently as he could to that part of the story, but he knew what came next and felt it was his turn to be the lecturer.

What neither of the friends knew was that another tour group was gathering on the other side of the wall. Those people couldn't see Lupus or Mannulus behind the large stone gate, but they could hear them, and they thought they were listening to a pair of tour guides.

Unaware that his audience had grown, Mannulus continued: 'The team kept uncovering houses and other buildings, but at first they weren't sure which settlement they were exploring. Finally a breakthrough came on 20 August 1763: the team uncovered an official inscription identifying the site as Pompeii.'

Lupus had been pacing, and butted in as soon as Mannulus paused for breath. 'Let's not forget something very important, Mannulus. None of Charles's excavations was intended to reveal and study Pompeii. Instead, Charles was happy for his men to collect vases, statues and other valuable objects so that the King could show them off. Having a kingdom full of such treasures would boost his reputation.'

'You're right. In a way those excavations weren't much better than the looting that had gone on in the past. And things didn't improve when the French showed up and got rid of Charles, or when the Austrians got rid of the French. It reminded me of Pompeii's early days with the Greeks against the Etruscans, who were against the Romans.'

Lupus and Mannulus were getting excited, and as they got

excited their voices became louder and louder. In fact, some of the people on the other side of the gate feared that the unseen tour guides might get into a fight. One mother took her young son aside and said, 'Climb up and have a look over the gate, darling. Tell us if we need to break up the argument.'

The little boy scrambled to the top and looked down. He was astounded and nearly fell off before climbing back down. He was out of breath but managed to say, 'It's a horse and a dog talking their heads off. They're not arguing – just excited.'

The adults chuckled and patted him on the back. One of them said, 'Oh, listen to that, the dog has started his lecture, or is it the horse?'

They laughed again and grew silent as they heard Lupus finishing his account: 'Of course things got much better – more organised and scientific – after Italy got rid of all those foreign rulers in 1861. For the first time a real archaeologist was put in charge of the excavations.'

Mannulus was happy to interrupt again: 'That was Giuseppe Fiorelli. And he finally imposed order on the site. Every discovery had to be recorded, and Fiorelli drew maps and diagrams of the town that was slowly emerging from the blanket of lava and ash.'

Lupus took a deep breath and smiled. He saw his chance to end the lecture on a high note: 'Not only did Fiorelli reveal the town that had been hidden for centuries, but his patient work seemed to bring some of the people and animals back to life. We now have casts of Pompeians who were frozen in time, captured at the moment their lives ended in the eruption.'

Mannulus nodded as Lupus gave a little bow. Meanwhile, the group on the other side of the gate began to applaud. They filed through the gate to congratulate the pair of tour guides but saw only a proud dog and horse, perfectly still.

'Hmm. The guides must have rushed off. It's only a pair of statues here now. Let's find where the guides have gone.' The group walked briskly away from the gate, with the little boy bringing up the rear. He looked back at the 'statues' and Lupus gave him a little wink.

BACK TO LIFE?

In 1863, Fiorelli noticed some cavities in the hardened blanket of lava and ash that covered Pompeii. He examined them closely and realised that each cavity was in the shape of a human body. As the ash and lava covering human bodies hardened, the bodies inside decomposed and eventually all traces disappeared. Fiorelli had his men fill the cavities with plaster. When the plaster hardened, they carefully removed the covering of hardened lava and ash. The result was a series of plaster casts of victims – a snapshot of the moment they were overcome during the eruption.

AD 79
MY THROAT'S BURNING.
VOLCANIC ASH BEGAN TO COVER HIM...
....BURYING HIS BODY AND SLOWLY TURNING TO STONE.

1863
POUR THE PLASTER INTO THE CAVITY BELOW.
IT'S SHAPED LIKE A MAN!
OH DEAR. IT'S A PLASTER CAST OF A VICTIM.

CHAPTER SIX
THE CITY RETURNS

Mannulus and Lupus had slept well, proud of their 'performance' by the gate the afternoon before. It was another beautiful morning, and about an hour before the site would be open to the public. The pair strolled casually into the Forum.

'You know, Mannulus, that episode yesterday – our secret lecture – made me think that we could become real guides. We wouldn't need headphones or notes because we've been here the whole time. We're eyewitnesses, really.'

'You're right. We saw Pompeii thriving, the dark clouds raining down ash and stone, the waves of lava... and the years of people sneaking in and looting or just leaving the city sleeping beneath its stony blanket.'

NEW TOOLS AND TECHNIQUES

Even the most sensitive tools and equipment to peel away layers of lava and ash can damage what lies beneath. Because of that risk, scientists are using new techniques to examine the evidence without damaging it. Some of these 'non-invasive' methods include using lasers, computers and cameras mounted on drones to record and analyse the remains. Even more worrying is the damage caused by the millions who visit Pompeii each year. Many of these visitors can now go on virtual tours of Pompeii, reducing traffic along the ancient streets.

'Mannulus, you're a poet. Now we need to practise something else: an explanation of what can be seen of Pompeii right now. You know, how much of Pompeii has been revealed, and maybe why we can't see more of it.'

THE PAST PREDICTING THE FUTURE?

The scientific attention devoted to Pompeii has revealed some startling information. One of the most dramatic discoveries is that Pompeii wasn't the first settlement to be destroyed by Vesuvius. An eruption around 1995 BC was much more powerful than the AD 79 event, laying waste to many Bronze Age communities in the same region as Pompeii. The scale of that earlier eruption has caused scientists to worry. It shows that the millions of people living around the Bay of Naples could be facing a devastating eruption at any time.

Mannulus took up the challenge. 'What people visit now is an archaeological site and not just some field of buried treasure. And it's really thanks to Giuseppe Fiorelli back in the 1800s that so much has been revealed.'

Lupus chimed in: 'One of the most important things he did was obvious, but no one had done it before. He divided the whole site into nine numbered sections. And the "insulae" – like modern blocks of flats – were also numbered, as well as the doors of the individual dwellings.'

'Yes! That way everyone knew where every item came from, as well as how different homes were built and decorated.'

Lupus continued, proud that the pair of them were bringing the story of Pompeii up to date: 'Archaeologists carried on Fiorelli's work, using his careful approach, through the twentieth century, although the site was damaged by bombs in the Second World War.'

'And they say that there are still some unexploded bombs around here, more than 70 years later!' Mannulus noted.

Lupus returned to the story: 'By the 1990s, about two-thirds of Pompeii had been excavated. Archaeologists and the general public then had an accurate idea of the size and layout. Overall, Pompeii covered 66 hectares (163 acres). Seven gates allowed people and traffic through the walls that ran 3 km (almost 2 miles) around the city.

'You and I know that the main street was Via Stabiana, the one that we took the other day when we followed the group from the theatre. It leads to the highest point in Pompeii, Vesuvius Gate.'

Mannulus had another point to make: 'I think we're forgetting about another big contribution made by all these excavations. Remember those teams who came to examine the different layers of lava with all those instruments? They were volcanologists, scientists who specialise in studying volcanoes.

Their research in Pompeii and Herculaneum has helped people understand how lava can travel at such high speeds, destroying communities with little or no warning.'

PYROCLASTIC FLOWS

For many years, scientists have agreed that the enormous 300°C (572°F) heat that lava reaches killed many Pompeii victims. But people still wondered whether lava could move fast enough to overtake people running away. Volcanologists have now observed similar eruptions, which trigger fast-moving 'rivers' of lava that race at speeds of up to 80 kph (50 mph). These outbursts, called pyroclastic flows or pyroclastic surges (depending on how much gas is mixed with the lava) probably sped down and blanketed Pompeii and anyone who was still there.

Lupus nodded. 'That's a real contribution, and maybe it could help prevent deaths and injuries in other volcanic eruptions – not just here, but all over the world.'

Both friends were full of pride at this point, and what had started out as a practice lecture now almost turned into a boast. Mannulus cleared his throat to announce: 'The United Nations recognises that Pompeii belongs to the whole world, and that the whole world should help preserve it. Being called a World Heritage Site is a huge honour, and helps raise money to continue studying and excavating Pompeii, but' – and his face became serious – 'in a way, Pompeii would be better off with less publicity.'

'I know what you mean,' agreed Lupus. 'Nearly three million people visit Pompeii each year. Three million! It's good that people want to learn about the past, or about volcanoes, or about Pompeii in particular, but having so many visitors has damaged much of the site.'

I THINK THIS IS WHERE THEY HAD A BIG MARKET.

WRONG. NOT JUST MARKETS. PEOPLE DID BUSINESS HERE, VOTED AND VISITED TEMPLES.

THANKS FOR REMINDING ME ABOUT THE TEMPLE. LOOK, IT'S OVER THERE!

I DIDN'T MENTION TEMPLES.

YOUR HEAD IS 2 METRES (6.6 FEET) ABOVE THE GROUND HERE. THE LAVA WAS MORE THAN 3 METRES (9.8 FEET) DEEP, WHICH IS HIGHER THAN THAT ROOF.

LOOK AT THIS DOG AND HORSE. THEY SEEM SO LIFELIKE!

THEY'RE THE BEST PART OF THE TOUR!

CLEVER CHILDREN. WHAT GOOD TASTE!

'And even without all those visitors, the ruins are becoming a little... ruined,' Mannulus pointed out. 'The blanket of ash and lava had preserved Pompeii for centuries. Being exposed to air and rain hasn't been good for many buildings.'

WINDOW TO THE PAST

UNESCO, the United Nations cultural organisation, recognises that Pompeii is one of the world's most important windows on to our past. By visiting and studying Pompeii we can learn a great deal about life nearly 2,000 years ago. Those same studies can help scientists understand more about the behaviour of active volcanoes like Vesuvius. In 1997 UNESCO made Pompeii a World Heritage site. That title means that UNESCO can team up with the Italian government to preserve Pompeii and fund research into the site.

Lupus agreed. 'Luckily the officials in charge of Pompeii are looking for ways of protecting it, without sending all those visitors away. New technology is leading Pompeii into the twenty-first century, and beyond. People can now arrive and take a virtual tour, without touching the delicate remains, or they can see Pompeii from a completely different angle, letting a drone take them through the entire site, including areas that are "off limits".'

'You know, Lupus, we just might still be around to show visitors what's what in another 2,000 years if they keep up the good work.'

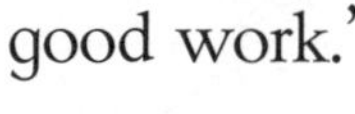

EPILOGUE

The pair of friends were once more in Pompeii's Forum, gazing across the excavation to the bay beyond, with Vesuvius behind them. The site was closed for the day and the sun was setting over the Bay of Naples.

'You know, Lupus, I sometimes imagine what it must be like to visit Pompeii for the first time. It's hard, I admit, considering we've known the place inside and out for about 2,000 years.

You could say that Pompeii holds no surprises for us. But do you think that a first-time visitor would be a bit overwhelmed by it all?'

'That depends,' Lupus answered after a little thought. 'If they knew nothing about the ancient world, then everything would be unfamiliar to them – the temples, the Forum, the Latin inscriptions, the style of clothing that you can see in the wall paintings. For them, the best thing would be to make several visits, learning about one subject at a time.'

'You're right. And for people who already know something about that period, Pompeii and Herculaneum give them a chance to see a moment frozen in time – the instant that normal life was snuffed out and preserved for the ages. Imagine the thrill of knowing a little Latin and seeing the everyday Latin scrawled as graffiti or election slogans on the preserved walls. Those are the sort of details that remain in people's memories long after they've visited these sites.'

'That's true, Lupus. And although visitors are shocked to see the casts of people whose lives ended in an instant, at the same time those casts bring life to the empty buildings. Visitors can imagine Pompeii to be a photograph taken at the moment normal life ended in a flash.'

Pompeii had certainly earned its place in history, according to the two friends. They'd spent the last few days re-living the events of the eruption nearly two thousand years earlier. As they stood, a light passed along a high wall marking the edge of the Forum. Another followed it, then others.

The two friends turned their gaze out to the sweeping bay. More lights swept past, then they heard a car horn and a radio playing music loudly. It was heavy traffic, streaming out of Naples in the evening rush hour. A junction of two busy roads lay just to the south of the quiet archaeological site. Manullus and Lupus looked down at the roads and followed the stream of cars northwards and around the bay to the bright lights of Naples. The coastal valley was starting to come alive with the lights from houses, public buildings and busy roads.

'Mannulus, I was just thinking. We talk a lot about the people in Pompeii being taken by surprise in AD 79. Well, did you know that three million people now live within 30 kilometres (18.6 miles) of Vesuvius?'

'That's a scary thought,' answered Mannulus as he turned his gaze to the volcano. 'By the way, does it look as though more smoke than normal is coming from the top of Vesuvius?'

'Oh, no! Here we go again.'

TIMELINE

BC

c. **760:** The Oscans, a people from central Italy, form five settlements along the Bay of Naples; one of them would become Pompeii.

c. **740:** The coastal settlements come under the influence of Greeks concentrated in the northern edge of the bay.

c. **700:** Etruscans, an advanced people from west-central Italy north of Rome, arrive in the area. At first they are happy just to trade with local people and to use ports and harbours for trade.

540: Pompeii becomes part of an Etruscan alliance in the area around the bay. Its population is about 2,000.

474: Greeks and their local allies in the area defeat the Etruscans at the Battle of Cumae, fought at sea.

c. **420:** Samnites, a people from central Italy who are allies of Rome, conquer the Greeks in the area around the Bay of Naples. Pompeii is one of the settlements to come under their control; it begins to grow and prosper.

343: Roman forces land at the mouth of the River Sarno and begin to extend their influence in the area.

c. 300 onwards: Pompeii came under overall Roman control but was allowed to keep many aspects of Samnite culture.

218–201: During the Second Punic War (Rome against its north African rival, Carthage) Pompeii refuses entry to Carthaginian General Hannibal, although several neighbouring cities welcome him.

c. 200 onwards: Rome defeats Carthage to gain full control over the Mediterranean region. It repays Pompeii's earlier loyalty by allowing it to trade widely within the Roman Empire.

90–89: Pompeii joins neighbouring cities in the Social War – their aim is to become full citizens of Rome. The Roman general Sulla defeats Rome's opponents and Pompeii becomes a colony. But its people are granted Roman citizenship after all.

31 BC onwards: Under Roman Emperor Augustus, Pompeii grows and many public buildings are erected.

AD

59: A violent riot in the Amphitheatre breaks out between locals and visitors from neighbouring Nuceria. Many people are badly injured. As a punishment for allowing this sort of behaviour, Emperor Nero bans entertainments in the Amphitheatre for ten years.

62: A serious earthquake damages much of Pompeii and neighbouring Herculaneum and Nuceria. Burning lamps fall from buildings during the earthquake, leading to serious damage from fires.

64: Emperor Nero and his wife Poppaea visit Pompeii, which is already rebuilding and expanding after the earthquake.

79: The eruption of Vesuvius takes place over two days either in August (based on Pliny the Younger's account) or October (based on recent discoveries):

Day I: The huge cloud of gas and pumice drifts across to Pompeii, raining down material for 18 hours. It is possible that most of Pompeii's 20,000 population escaped during this time because only 1,150 bodies have been found.

Day 2: Pyroclastic flows of dense ash clouds and lava race down the slopes and into the city, toppling buildings. Neighbouring Herculaneum escapes the worst of the cloud but is also buried by the pyroclastic flows. Like Pompeii it lies beneath a blanket of ash and lava up to 6 m (20 feet) deep.

79–80: Emperor Titus leads efforts to help the survivors and visits the site twice within a year. He calls for rebuilding but very little happens.

80 onwards: After some survivors return, hoping to find some of their belongings, only looters spend any time in Pompeii. Over time the city is almost forgotten.

471–473: Vesuvius erupts and deposits more lava on Pompeii.

512: Another eruption adds even more lava.

1592: The crew working for architect Domenico Fontana uncover part of Pompeii while digging an underground canal. Fontana decides against any exploration.

1748: King Charles III of Naples supports an excavation at Pompeii.

1806–1815: While the region is under French control, up to 700 men continue excavations at Pompeii.

1860: King Victor Emmanuel II of newly independent Italy appoints Giuseppe Fiorelli to lead the excavations at Pompeii.

1863 onwards: Fiorelli imposes order and discipline at the excavation, aiming to preserve as much as possible.

1920s–1950s: The last great excavations take place at Pompeii, as people also become concerned about preserving what has been exposed.

1939–1945: Pompeii suffers damage from fighting during the Second World War.

1980: An earthquake in southern Italy damages much of the site.

1997: Pompeii becomes a UN World Heritage Site.

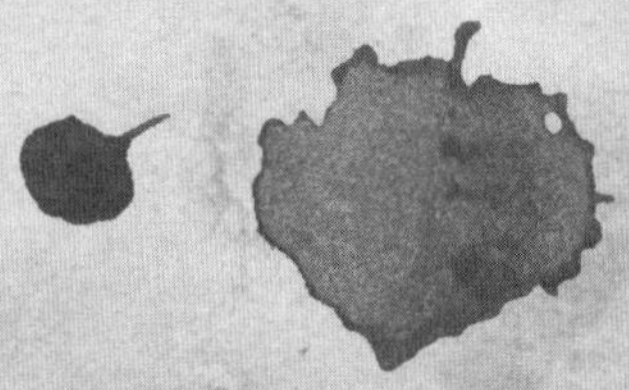

GLOSSARY

Accuracy: Being free of mistakes or errors.

Alliance: An agreement between two or more parties to support each other in case of attack.

Amphitheatre: A round or oval public building with rows of seats rising from a central, open area.

Amphorae: Two-handled pots (singular: amphora) with a narrow neck and used to hold liquids or grains.

Arc: A curving shape, like part of a circle.

Archaeologist: A person who studies human history by examining objects that have been found at excavations.

Barbarian: A person from a different place or background that others consider to be primitive or even violent.

Basilica: A large hall or building used in ancient Rome as a law court or for public gatherings.

Brooding: Concentrating on a single idea, often in a sad or worried way.

Bustling: Busy and full of life.

Caldarium: The hottest room in a Roman bath; hot air from a furnace would flow beneath the floor to warm a pool of water where bathers would wash.

Canter: A quick pace of movement for a horse, but not as fast as a gallop.

Cast: An object formed by pouring liquid into a hollow mould; the liquid hardens into the shape of the mould.

Catastrophe: A disaster with wide-ranging effects.

Cobbled: Paved with stones.

Colony: A territory governed by another country.

Colosseum: A large amphitheatre or other building used to stage entertainments or combat.

Combat: Fighting between two opponents.

Crater: A circular area of coastline or land, usually shaped like a bowl with a rim; the inside of a volcano is often shaped like a crater.

Crisis: An unpredictable situation that could produce worrying results.

Crossroads: A place where two or more roads meet; it can also describe a place where people with different backgrounds come together.

Decomposed: Decayed and broken down into simpler elements.

Earthquake: A shaking or other violent movement of the Earth's surface, often linked to volcanic activity.

Eruption: When material blocked inside an object (such as a volcano) suddenly bursts out with explosive force.

Etruscans: An advanced group of people who controlled much of western Italy from around 900 BC before expanding to include parts of southern Italy by 750 BC.

Excavation: An area that has been dug out of the ground; often used to describe an area that has been dug to reveal evidence of the past.

Extinct: Something that no longer exists.

Forum: The central place in ancient Roman towns and cities where business and government matters were conducted.

Frigidarium: The coldest room in a Roman bath. The bathers would plunge into cold water there after having passed through the caldarium (hot room) and tepidarium (warm room).

Garum: A strong-tasting, salty fish sauce that was popular in many ancient lands along the Mediterranean Sea.

Gladiator: A warrior who would take part in combats, sometimes to the death, in the ancient world.

Graffiti: Anything scratched or written on a public wall, usually by someone who had not been hired to do so.

Granary: A building designed to store grain.

Harvest: Crops when they are ripe; also the action of gathering ripe crops.

Heritage: Something from the past that has been carefully preserved.

Hygiene: Practices and actions that promote health and cleanliness.

Insulae: The plural form of the Latin word 'insula', meaning a large building divided into many dwellings like modern flats.

Lava: Melted rock that erupts from a volcano.

Looting: The theft of valuable items from a tomb or other archaeological site.

Magma: Hot, liquid rock that is beneath the Earth's surface but rises up through volcanoes.

Non-invasive: Designed in a way that does not disturb other objects.

Pedestal: The base of a statue or other large display.

Plate: One of the large sections of the Earth's surface that slides slowly, sometimes colliding with other plates to cause earthquakes or volcanic eruptions.

Plume: A shape that resembles a wispy feather.

Pomegranate: A type of juicy, reddish fruit that contains

many seeds and which grows throughout the Mediterranean region, including Pompeii.

Population: The overall number of people living in a certain area.

Pumice: Lava that has hardened to become a type of lightweight rock.

Pyroclastic flow: A fast-moving mixture of lava, gas and ash that flows along the ground during some volcanic eruptions.

Roman Empire: A huge area of Europe, North Africa and western Asia that was controlled by Rome from 27 BC to 476 AD. It reached its greatest size in 117 AD.

Scrawled: Written quickly and often messily.

Second World War: A war fought in Europe, Africa and Asia between 1939 and 1945 and involving more than 60 countries.

Settlement: A permanent dwelling place.

Spectators: People who watch a sporting or entertainment performance.

Strigil: A scraping tool made of metal and used in ancient times to wipe sweat and dirt off a bather's skin.

Suffocated: To die through lack of air.

Sweeping: Extending over a long distance.

Tepidarium: The warm room of a Roman bath. The bathers would work up a sweat before entering and then clean themselves in this room with a strigil before moving on to the caldarium and frigidarium.

Tremor: A small earthquake, often occurring just before or after a more powerful earthquake.

United Nations: An international organisation founded in 1945 to promote world peace and understanding.

Villa: A country house, which is often large and luxurious.

Volcanologist: A scientist who specialises in the study of volcanoes.

Wisp: A thin trace of smoke, cloud or other floating material.

INDEX